BUDGET COMPUTERS

Triston Derbidge

Photos by Triston Derbidge
Editor LeAnn Skrzynski

Trademarks

HP®, ASUS®, Lenovo®, Acer®, Dell®, Apple®, Amazon®, Android®, Oracle®, Adobe®, Mac®, Linux®, Windows®, YouTube®, Google®, NirSoft®, CORTANA®, and other brand names mentioned within are trademarks of their respective owners and are in no way affiliated with the author(s) of this book.

Budget Computers is acknowledged to be the intellectual property of its author(s).

Disclaimer

By receiving this book, you agree to release the author(s), illustrators, collaborators, editors, photographers, and publishers of liability from any harm and damage, physical or otherwise, as a result of reading this book.

We all have a hero and a villain, a genius and a fool, in our hearts. Indulge them equally and the world won't be any better… but it won't be any worse.

-Nicolas Carpenter

Contents at a Glance

Useful Information

Social Engineering Attacks

Social engineering attacks are security attacks designed to panic the target and persuade them into revealing sensitive information. The most popular attacks, in my experience, are pretexting and phishing (pronounced “fishing”).

Pretexting

Pretexting usually involves fraud where the attacker pretends to need information to confirm the identity of the person he is talking to. After inciting panic then establishing trust with the target as having the solution, the attacker will ask a series of questions designed to gather key information such as social security numbers, mother’s maiden name, birth dates, and account numbers. This is usually done by phone. The best I have experienced was a phone call from a man pretending to be from the Department of Justice. The man claimed he was calling because the government believes my bank accounts were being used to launder money, and that he requires my bank account information to verify that I was not involved. Obviously, if the government had the slightest thought that my bank accounts were being used to launder money, SWAT would be kicking in my door with assault rifles. The last thing they would do is send me a friendly phone call to warn me of suspicion.

Phishing (fishing)

Phishing is attempting to acquire sensitive information such as credit card information, user account information, as well as encouraging harmful actions. The attacker will often present themselves as a representative of a trustworthy establishment such as a bank or company. This type of action was given the name phishing because less-then-well-intentioned people attempt to bait victims into revealing sensitive information. The most common attempts I have seen at phishing have been calls from people claiming to be from Microsoft telling me they have noticed I've contracted a virus on my personal computer (PC). They proceed to tell me to download software to resolve the issue. Often the software they want you to download will contain a trojan horse (malware disguised as innocent software) and by downloading the software, your system will actually become infected.

In conclusion, if you are contacted in this or similar manner, do not panic! Take a moment to use common sense. Social engineering attacks have very serious and very real life-altering effects on its victims. A cool head and a little knowledge can turn a serious situation into a good story. It will also help to know there are hefty fines for violating the Do Not Call list and bad news is always free: anyone willing to exchange bad news for sensitive information never has good intentions. Additional information on social engineering attacks can be found online.

Anti-Malware / Anti-Virus

Malware comes in many variations: from ransomware and rootkits to trojan horses and worms. Variations of these variations are constantly evolving - for this reason it's important to have reliable anti-virus (AV) / anti-malware software and keep it up to date. Both free and paid software can be found to suit your needs. One common misconception that surrounds AV software is the length of protection, particularly on brand new computers. Most computers come with a free TRIAL AV software: note the word "trial", as in temporary. After the trial period, people will often ignore the warnings to buy the full software or renew their current subscription. Although they have antivirus software, it is no longer updating to protect against constant changes to malicious software - yet consumers mistakenly blame the software for their own negligence. Always be sure any subscriptions and protective software are up to date for the best protection of personal information.

The Internet

The Internet is a powerful tool, not just for social media and marketing. Any errors or issues you may come across can more than likely be found online: all you need is Internet access, an error code, or brief description of the problem. A simple search will pull up a whole buffet of information and even videos of possible solutions. Keep in mind that not every experience is exactly the same, so it may take a moment to find the solution that best fits your problem.

Cloud Computing

Cloud computing is the ability to use services provided by different entities such as Google, Microsoft, and Amazon, that allows us to save and share data, perform tasks, and use software without having to store data and install applications (apps) in a local device. Because data is stored on remote drives, they can easily be accessed by many different devices, including smartphones, laptops, and gaming consoles while remaining completely secure. There are both free and paid services available (such as Google Drive and Amazon Prime music) which allows you to make and modify documents and spreadsheets, and listen to music over the Internet.

Parental Control

While the subject of many intense arguments, parental control software is a useful protection tool. In a lot of virus cases, malicious software is accidentally downloaded while someone was browsing the Internet, even with innocent intentions. Parental control software is not only a safeguard against dangerous sites, it can be useful to filter words and sites from a search, monitor activity, or even limit time spent online. If this concept is interesting to you, take a moment to research parental control programs online. There will be a great number of options, each with different functions to suit your needs. There will, of course, be free and paid services, but keep in mind, what's right for you may not be right for others.

Passwords

If your password is QWERTY1234, you're not even remotely near a safe zone. A strong password is a lot like a good car: it keeps you safe as you move from A to Z. There is a list of rules to follow when selecting a strong password:

1. Avoid phrases you use often – if you are known around town as the guy who says, "Howdy", it will not make a strong password.
2. Do not use words right out of a dictionary. Hackers often use dictionary words as attempts to guess a password.
3. Use at least ten characters - including numbers, upper- and lower-case letters, and special characters (exclamation point, asterisk, forward slash, and so on).
4. Avoid sequences. Patterned characters - such as 12345, qwerty, and abcde - are easy to remember but also easy to guess.
5. Try to make a password that can be remembered but is unrelated to you - much like common phrases, known information about you can easily be guessed as a password. For a person with little interest in astronomy, a strong, unrelated

password might be "@StronoMy2souP!" Be sure to make use of different characters, symbols, and letters.

Power Surges / Outages

As you have no doubt discovered, power problems can have devastating effects on computers. It is always a good idea to buy a strong surge protector to plug your electronics into - not just desktops and laptops, but printers, monitors, and even TVs. If surges are a common occurrence near you, surge protectors will slowly lose their ability to block spikes in electricity yet still appear to be working. If you're concerned for the safety of anything connected to a protector, it would be a good idea to replace the protector after five to ten surges. The reason for this section is because surge damage is very common and typically difficult for people with low tech experience to diagnose. With that in mind, if you happen to have a device that refuses to power on after the last thunderstorm, there may be a very easy solution.

For laptops, the large brick-shaped object inline on the charge cable (known as an inverter because it turns 120VAC to about 19VDC) is also the first line of defense. A spike of electricity will often ruin the inverter and leave the laptop unharmed but if left powered on, the laptop battery will run empty and need to be recharged which is why most people think the surge caused irreparable damage to the device. Try to find a matching charger that was not plugged in during the storm and power it up. If you don't have a spare, the best option is eBay where a replacement can often be found for under $20: much cheaper than assuming the whole laptop needs replaced. Keep in mind, a laptop can be damaged by a surge but it's more likely just the charger.

For desktops, you will notice the lack of an inverter in the power cord because the process of converting 120VAC to 12VDC happens in the power supply unit (PSU) inside the case. The easiest route is to simply take the PC to a local computer repair shop and have them install a new power supply. If you would prefer to save money and do this yourself, first follow the guide lines from the section "Preparing for the Upgrade". Once set up, open the case and begin tracing all the connections from the power supply. You may have to cut a few zip ties then proceed to disconnect all power cables. There should be one cable to the hard drive, one to the disk drive, two or so to the motherboard, plus one or so to fans inside the case. Remember where these connections are because they will have to be reconnected in the same manner to the new power supply; pictures or even hand drawn diagrams will be helpful.

Once all connections are removed, the power supply should be held in place by about three screws on the back panel. Remove these screws and slide the PSU out of the case (there may also be a clip that holds the PSU in place). On the PSU, there will be a label with all of the electrical ratings. Find the wattage rating for the PSU, which is usually 300-500 watts. When selecting a new power supply, a higher wattage can be used safely if a matching one cannot be found, but be sure to never use a lower-rated PSU because it will definitely cause damage to the computer. Any brand is fine, the importance is the physical size. Depending on the form factor of your computer, select an ATX or MicroATX with a wattage equal to or higher than the old PSU, that fits your budget.

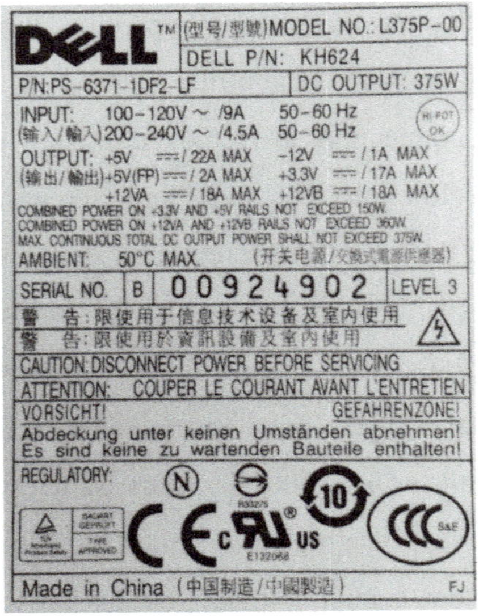

Figure 1.1 PSU Label

It may help to know that a desktop will not draw more wattage then it needs, so a larger PSU is perfectly safe. With the new power supply, to do the install work backwards from removal, slide the new unit into place, secure with three or so screws, run and secure cables with zip ties, and reconnect cables to the HDD, DVD drive, motherboard, and other peripherals that require a connection. While this process may sound difficult while reading, it should be easy to perform (YouTube videos can also be helpful). It will take a fair amount of time: remember to be patient, make sure no cables get snagged or caught, and do not block air flow from fans.

Note from the Author

Caution: Do not attempt to open the casing of the PSU unit – it contains capacitors that will likely be holding a deadly charge long after being disconnected from power.

Helpful Supply List

- Anti-Static Grounding Bracelet
- Mini Assorted Screwdriver Kit
- Plastic Tweezers (avoid metal unless you wear the grounding bracelet)
- Compartmental Organizer
- Plastic Pry Tools
- Compressed Gas Duster
- Soft Cloths (microfiber material works best)
- Anti-Static Cleaner (TV screen cleaner works well)
- Operating System Media (necessary for upgrading OS)
- Product Key (Should be included with OS media if purchased from a legitimate vendor)
- Hard Drive: Desktop size 3.5" / Laptop size 2.5" (necessary for upgrading or replacing an old hard drive)
- System Specific Memory (RAM) (Refer to Step 3 Matching Components, size differs between laptop and desktop. You will need to match

revision and clock speed; storage size may be higher than current RAM)

This list should prove helpful when shopping for upgrade components. Not all of these items will be necessary depending on the extent of your upgrades but please read or, at a minimum, skim through the book to determine what you need before placing an order to avoid multiple purchasing (and shipping costs).

Pretext

To most people, buying a new computer means pulling out the plastic and racking up another five years of debt. To me, that's just CRAZY! The average life expectancy for a computer is only about seven years. However, today it has never been easier to pick a computer to match your lifestyle and keep your budget intact. And by computer, I include desktops, laptops, and tablets.

The first step is to determine what you need based on your lifestyle.

The second step is learning what to look for and shop around for a couple of prospects.

The third step is to determine user upgrades that each prospect can easily, and cost effectively, utilize.

The fourth step is to purchase your new computer and perform upgrades - yes, by yourself!

The fifth step is learning how to care for and preserve the life of your new computer.

The sixth step is to figure out what to do with your old computer.

By purchasing this book, you will gain the knowledge to make an informed decision when buying new computers: not just now, but in the future as well. You will acquire a few skills to get the most out of your money and your computer, plus understand the importance of proper care and handling of computers. I will explain in detail how to perform some simple, yet amazingly helpful, upgrades. You will also be able to utilize video-sharing and tech sites, where you can get the most out of other people's experiences. Along the way, I will explain certain technical terms such as RAM, DIMM, SODIMM, X32 Bit (X86), X64 Bit, CAS latency and how to match RAM.

1

Determine what you need based on your lifestyle

(The power you need for the life you lead)

This is one of the most important steps to buying a new computer. Just like your car and house, your computer should represent your personality. The first thing you should look at before buying a new computer is your lifestyle. But remember, if you want more power then you actually need (like me), you don't need to spend a fortune to get it.

If you're planning to purchase a computer for a child or young adult or even your first computer, it doesn't need any special features like Adobe Photoshop or Oracle's VirtualBox. Deciding on a simple computer with 2 gigabytes (GB) of RAM and around 120GBs of hard drive storage space and the most current operating system (OS) would set you up for the technologies of today.

If you typically use your current computer to surf the web, send emails, and watch YouTube videos, 4 to 6GBs of RAM, 250-500GBs of hard drive space, and the most current version of OS would suit your needs quite well. This is also the most common configuration used in low technical (tech) manufacturing companies. Most users that choose this configuration also typically use Microsoft's (paid) office software, including Microsoft OneDrive (free Cloud storage), and OneNote (free Cloud-based notes) - all of which require a Microsoft account (free to create), or Google Drive, which has similar document and spreadsheet capabilities in a free-to-use Cloud-based format. I'll let you decide which services are right for you. While Cloud storage can be used, if you like to have a lot of music and videos on your device, the bigger hard drive space, the better.

For photo, music, and video editing, 8 to 16GBs of RAM and 500GBs to 1 terabyte (TB) of hard drive space is more adequate. However, if these are the kinds of features you're looking for in a computer, you can also make use of Microsoft and Google Cloud storage, as well as external hard drives and inexpensive memory upgrades.

Gamers utilize anywhere from 16 to 128GBs of RAM and typically 256GB to 6TBs of solid state hard drive space, as well as liquid and Peltier cooling. These types of computers are usually very expensive to purchase or are custom built to meet the high-end needs of modern gamers. While gamers often use the same variations of Cloud storage and operating systems, due to their high expense and the fact that they do not fall under the category of "Budget Computers", these types of systems will NOT be covered in this book.

And now onto the next step, finding a few prospects.

2

Learning what to look for

(Shop around for a couple of prospects)

When you're looking for a new computer, it helps to know where to look just as much as what to look for. While we've all seen the selection in big department stores, personally, I do NOT suggest this route: department stores typically charge significantly more for devices you could purchase online. If you get coupons to these types of stores or enjoy a brawl on Black Friday, it is completely possible to find a good deal at a brick and mortar business, but not always likely.

The most common place to look for computers is, of course, the manufacturer's websites.

Such as:

Lenovo www.lenovo.com/us/en/

HP (Hewlett Packard) www.hp.com/

Acer www.acer.com/ac/en/US/content/home

ASUS www.asus.com/US/

Apple www.apple.com/

Dell www.dell.com/en-us/

Each company has advantages. HP allows you to customize most computers before you purchase, but this usually costs more than performing the upgrades yourself. Lenovo and Acer typically provide full specs which will help inform the user of upgrade types you might want to perform on your own.

You can also save a few bucks by searching other tech-friendly sites, such as:

Amazon www.Aamazon.com/

Amazon Warehouse Deals

www.Aamazon.com/b?ie=UTF8&node=10158976011

Newegg www.newegg.com/

eBay www.ebay.com/

On these sites, particularly Amazon Warehouse Deals, you can find open-box, used and refurbished computers, as well as last year's models. While you may not like the sound of that, always remember that it's a good (and inexpensive) way to find a first computer for a child, young teen or even just something to play with. Along with affordable computers, there is also usually a large selection of used RAM chips. While some folks may warn against buying used RAM, their solid-state build makes them a very resilient piece of equipment that should last a long time, at a very friendly price.

Latest Versions of Operating Systems

It helps to know the newest versions of operating systems out today so you can make an informed decision on newer products. Current OS are as follows:

1. **Microsoft Windows OS** (this is the typical OS for personal computers)
   a. Windows 10 (the newest version of Windows OS, released in 2015).
   b. There is no Windows 9, due to name-pathing reasons.
   c. Windows 8.1 (an upgraded version of Windows 8, which was a fairly big flop) released in 2013.
   d. Windows 7, released in 2009 (not as new as Windows 8.1 or 10 but typically preferred over newer OS due to its simplicity - even brand new computers will be sold with this version of OS).

All versions of Microsoft's OS require a product key which is located on a Certificate of Authenticity (COA). This COA also lists the version of OS and is usually located on the bottom of the device or under battery compartments. Windows 8 and up have an embedded product key which cannot be found on a COA, but can be located by downloading NirSoft's Lightweight Procukey (free to use product key location software), which is very handy if you need to reinstall your OS.

Figure 2.1 Microsoft COA

2. Apple OSX

a. OS X 10.12 Sierra (the newest version of Apple's OSX) released in 2016
b. OS X 10.11 El Capitan released in 2015
c. OS X 10.10 Yosemite, released in 2014
d. OS X 10.9 Maverick, released in 2013

Typically, if the Mac system supports the higher versions, the update is usually free if you have an Apple account. Usually the biggest difference between the versions of OSX are security updates.

3. Android OS

a. Nougat 7.0, released in 2016
b. Marshmallow 6.0, released in 2015
c. Lollipop 5.0, released in 2014

d. KitKat 4.0, released in 2013

Due to its open source system, the same version of Android will look and feel differently between manufacturers, who have made slight changes to better suit their devices.

Compile Your List

Now that you know what to look for, you can start by searching keywords like: "laptop", "desktop", "Mac" or "tablets". Usually you'll find you can refine your search parameters on the left of the page, where you select what operating system, screen size, memory, and hard drive space you want to see. I don't suggest setting a search priority based on RAM - I will be explaining how you can upgrade the RAM on your system by yourself which will save a considerable amount of money, however, it is usually more cost effective to purchase a system with the amount of hard drive space suited to you. Hard drives are typically more complicated and expensive to upgrade. At the end of this book, I will go into detail on how to upgrade a hard drive. While you're searching around, be sure to keep a list with the name of the system, as well as the site you found the device and its specifications.

Example:

Amazon.com

Lenovo Ideapad 100 15.6-Inch Laptop $249.74

New

4GB DDR3L 1333MHz RAM 500GB HDD

Intel Pentium processor

Windows 10 Home 64-Bit

Max RAM:

Newegg.com

HP 255 G4 15.6" Notebook $287.99 New

4GB DDR3L 1600MHz RAM 500GB HDD

AMD A6 processor Windows Home 10 64-Bit

Max RAM:

Dell E6220 $139.00 Refurbished

4GB DDR3 1333MHz RAM 250GB HDD

Intel Core i5

Windows 7 Home Prem. 64-Bit

Max RAM:

It's also good to know that when you are determining whether to buy used /refurbished or new, most new and refurbished computers will have some sort of warranty (usually for the first year that will cover manufacturer defaults, as well as refurbished defaults, but every company has different policies). Adding these devices into your shopping cart on that site will allow for a quick return to that device while you're shopping around.

While you're making this list, don't limit yourself initially, but you shouldn't write a phone book either. A list of ten or twelve is not ridiculous: it's good to have options because you will be narrowing this list by cutting out the devices that might either be too expensive to purchase or upgrade, or just won't fit into your lifestyle.

3

Determine which user upgrades each prospect can easily and cost effectively utilize

Once your list is compiled, you'll want to search each device's capabilities and determine their full potential specification (specs), as well as the price for those upgrades. Usually you can just type the computer name as well as the word "specs" into your search engine and it will pull up multiple sites that meet your search parameters. I personally prefer CNET, as I've found that it provides the most information on devices I'm interested in upgrading or refurbishing. Most manufacturer's sites will usually provide more in-depth specifications for the devices. These specification sites will not only provide a list of typical and possible configurations, but also customer and tech specialist reviews. These lists usually include:

- General Information: System brand, Windows version, form factor (desktop/netbook/notebook)
- Processor/chipset Information: CPU name, number of cores, cache, 64-bit computing
- RAM: Memory speed, configuration features, technology, installed size
- Storage: Interface
- Memory: Max supported size, technology, speed, form factor, slot quantity, empty slots

While you're researching each device, you'll notice a difference in form factor between desktop RAM and laptop RAM:

SODIMM (used in laptops and most very small space-saving desktops)

Figure 3.1 SODIMM

DIMM (used in desktops and servers)

Figure 3.2 DIMM

(There is a significant size and pin difference between the two)

While you are researching all the devices on your list, be sure you're adding the price and where you found the upgrade components. Also, be aware that most tablets, as well as newer Mac computers, cannot be upgraded.

Matching Components

One critical piece of advice you must follow is matching the RAM exactly to the systems requirements. The only variables that are allowed are brand, GB size and CAS latency. The form factor, DDR version, speed, and voltage MUST match. Though it is possible to install a DDR3L in a DDR3 memory slot, DDR3 cannot be placed in a DDR3L slot. Doing so can cause damage to your computer and components. The easiest method is to simply match the following items:

a. DDR Version or Revision
    1. DDR
    2. DDR2
    3. DDR3
    4. DDR4

I find it best to simply buy low voltage (DDR#L) RAM because it can be installed in both 1.5V and 1.3V slots without adverse effects on price or performance.

b. Clock Speed
    1. 1066
    2. 1333

3. 1600
4. 2400

Some RAM chips will not be marked, for example, as DDR4 2400, but as PC4 19200. This is a form of longhand for RAM. Searching the PC numbers will bring up the same results as searching the DDR numbers.

(When it comes to RAM, more GBs and less CAS latency are better.)

By this point you'll notice some prospective computers are more upgrade friendly then others, and you should be able to cut a few off your list that you don't believe will be best for your lifestyle or are not cost-friendly.

Collect Necessary Accessories

Before you begin to open your computer, it's best to have a few tools to keep you and your computer out of harm's way and make the job much simpler. The following tools can usually be found at Amazon.com, your local hardware store, or the electronic section at most stores.

1. Grounding Bracelet (to avoid electric static discharge)
2. Mini Assorted Screwdriver Kit
3. Plastic Tweezers (metal will work if you are well grounded)
4. Compartmental Organizer (for retaining little screws and parts)
5. Plastic Pry Tool (believe it or not, most people typically use an old credit card or gift card for this purpose)

Some of these tools may not seem important but are a very helpful when opening a computer for any reason and are typically inexpensive. All these items combined should cost about $25 in addition to the cost of your computer.

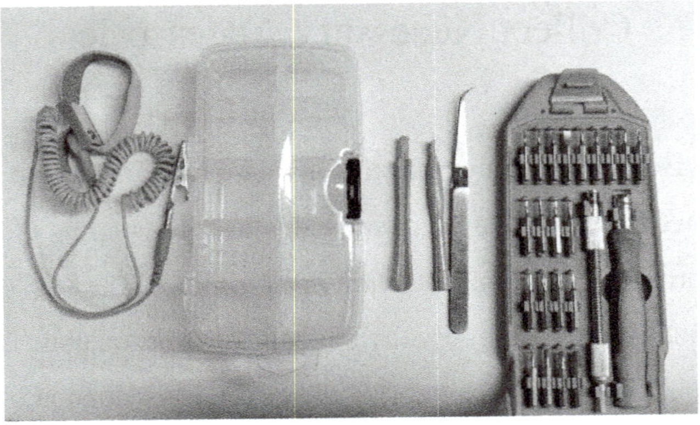

Figure 3.3 Necessary Tools

4

Purchase your new computer and perform upgrades - yes, by yourself!

You are nearly ready to purchase your new computer after determining the last few computer options. If you haven't narrowed it to one due to price and upgrade similarities it's best to look at what brands and versions of computers are more user upgrade-friendly than others (ease of access). Certain brands make it extremely easy for users to upgrade their computers, while others make it nearly impossible for even highly trained IT technicians to repair on their own. It's important to know that essentially all desktops can be opened and have field-replaceable components, whereas all tablets require a high level of technical knowledge to perform even simple repairs and cannot be upgraded. The following list pertains to laptops.

The most user upgradable brands I have come across are:

- Lenovo
- Acer
- ASUS (though they typically frown on user alterations)

The least upgrade-friendly I've seen are:

- Apple (a great product, but newer models cannot be opened by users and the average IT technician)
- HP (which followed the recent trend of "inoperable" computers)

Keep in mind that the more compact a device, the less likely it can be upgraded. Thankfully, the trend of inoperable computers is slowing down but shows no sign of stopping.

Also, important information to have is the top vender market shares:

As of 2016: As of 2012

Top 6 vendors by numbers of units shipped, 2016			Greenpeace Rating
Rank	Manufacturer	Gartner	Out of 10
1	Lenovo	21.2%	3.9
2	HP	20.8%	5.7
3	Dell	16.0%	4.6
4	Asus	7.2%	-
5	Apple	7.1%	4.5
6	Other	27.0%	-

The Greenpeace rating system is based on how "green" or environmentally friendly the products are. The higher the rating the better.

By now, you should have enough background to decide on which computer you want and will purchase with the likelihood of living with it for the next five years.

Preparing for the Upgrade

Now that you have your computer and upgrade components, I find it best to power on the computer, go through the start up process, and perform a few remedial tasks to ensure the computer is functioning properly before tampering inside the computer. To get started, it's best to set up a clean, dust-free, and well-lit area with plenty of table space. The start up process takes a fair amount of time - usually about thirty to forty-five minutes – so you can save some time by skipping any updates the computer may need until you have finished the upgrade.

Because of their increasing popularity, I'll be explaining the basics of upgrading laptops first, with desktops to follow shortly after. Keep in mind, most laptops vary in design and MAY require different methods of disassembly as a result.

The first step you'll want to take is to power off the device and place it in the center of the table closest to you. Now place your tools (mini screw driver set, compartment organizer, etc.) on the table so they are well within reach but not in your way. Be sure that all the screws you remove are placed into the compartment organizer as you go along and labeled in such a way that you will remember exactly where they go, as not all screws are the same size. It's best to make sure you're not near water or anything that could product excessive static (Tesla coils and Van de Graaff generators included), although your grounding bracelet will help relieve static issues.

Next, place the strap from the grounding bracelet around your wrist and button the cord to the strap. Normally the clip end would hook to an unpainted part of the computer case but laptops rarely have such a spot. You should be able to pull the alligator clip off the end of the cord and plug the round end into the **Ground** slot on a wall outlet or less recommended, on a grounded extension cord. The grounding slot (the half oblong hole on the bottom of a 3-prong power outlet) on an electrical outlet does not have any electrical connection of its own; it is simply used to let excess current leave the circuit in a safe manner by connecting a single copper wire to a piece of unpainted metal inside the wall.

The purpose for the grounding bracelet is to remove excess static buildup from your body, away from the computer and components that could be damaged by electrostatic discharge (ESD). While it may not seem like it, static can deal real damage to electrical components. Static must be over 3,000 Volts for a person to hear a shock, 5,000 Volts to feel the shock, and 8,000 to see the shock; the reason this is relevant is because it only takes 10 Volts of static electricity to completely ruin a computer. That means if you happen to be playing with a Taser®, put it down while you're performing the upgrade.

Now flip over the laptop so the bottom of the case is facing upward, and remove the battery, if possible. There are typically two types of laptops: the first has one to three different bottom covers that can be removed. The second is one that doesn't appear to have any covers that can be removed and the whole bottom cover is a single piece - with this type, you'll have to do a little more work.

NEVER force anything together or apart; doing so will only result in damage.

The upgrade
Laptops
A. One to Three Piece Covers

If your laptop has at least one removable panel, look on the panel for an "M" or small icon that looks like a memory chip. Go ahead and remove all screws that are holding the panel in place. This may be three or four screws or even a single screw that was hidden by the battery.

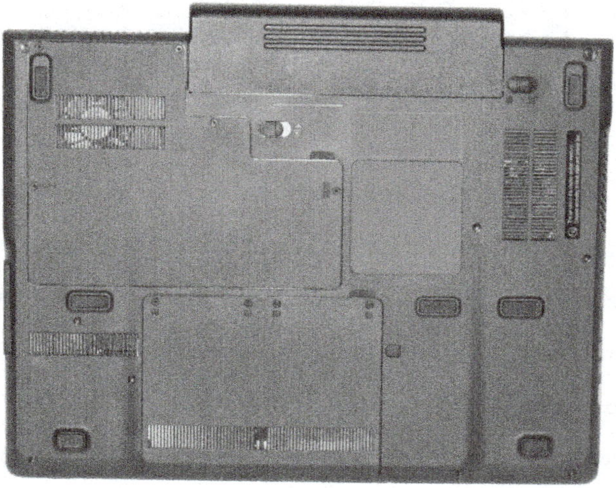

Figure 4.1 1-3 Piece Laptop Bottom

Once you've removed the screws, lift, or slide off the cover to reveal the RAM slots. There are usually two slots. However, in a few older laptops there will be one slot on the bottom and one under the keyboard itself.

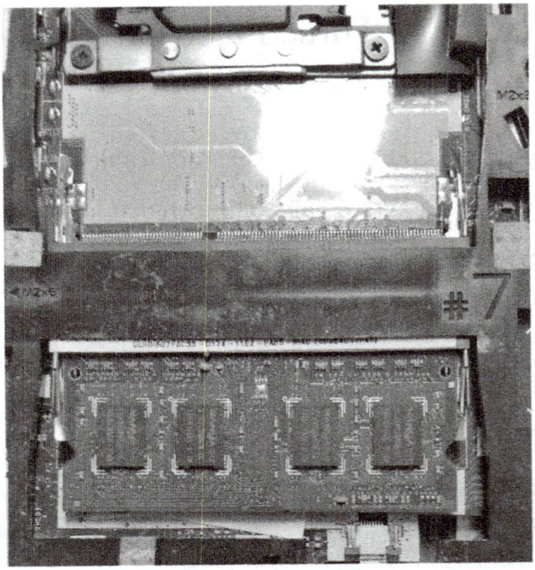

Figure 4.2 SODIMM SLOTS

If you're replacing both chips, use both index fingers and pull outward on the two outer metal clamps that hold the chip(s) in place to release the installed memory and gently pull outward at the same angle as the chip. Place the chip in a safe place out of the way. (Skip this step if you're simply adding a chip to the existing RAM. If you purchased a two pack of RAM, it's best to use the set because matching components function better then mix and match).

Now open the package of the new chips and gently remove one chip from the package without touching any of the gold contacts; it's best to hold the chip by the side edges to prevent force and static damage. Line up the notch in the chip with the notch in slot A and gently place the chip in the slot at a 45° angle. Once the chip has slipped in the slot as far as it can, use one finger and lightly push straight down on the chip until it locks in place.

Figure 4.3 45° Angle SODIMM

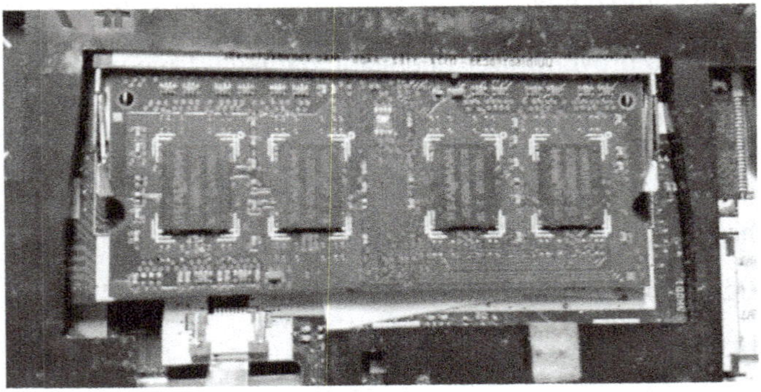

Figure 4.4 Locked in SODIMM

Once you have finished installing the chip, you can replace any covers that were removed for access and the battery, then start the device. If everything was done properly and with care the device should start right up. Once the system is booted, press the Windows key + R; when a dialog box opens, type CMD for another box to open as a command line. Here type MSINFO32, to open a third window displaying all the information about the device, such as the OS name, system name, model, and manufacturer, as well as the physical memory installed and Available Physical Memory. Note that the Available Physical Memory will be lower than the Installed Physical Memory which is expected since certain processes and functions require and claim the amount of memory they need to work properly. If the system does not read the full amount of RAM that has been installed, your OS software may be 32 Bit. A clean install to 64 Bit software will allow the system to access the full amount of RAM (please refer to the Data Destruction and Updating Hard Drives section of this book) or a RAM chip may be faulty or not locked in place.

B. Single Piece Cover

For this configuration, there is a lot more work required for the upgrade. Follow the pre-upgrade instructions from above chapter "Preparing for the Upgrade". Once you are ready, observe how many screws there are and be aware of the fact they may not all be the same size (usually the screws from the corners will be longer or wider than the rest). There may also be hidden screws underneath the rubber feet on each cover of the device - if you remove these and cannot get them back on, I recommend a small amount of double-sided tape which can be found at most convenient stores or online shopping websites for very little. A VERY SMALL amount of Superglue® would also do the trick, but also make it that much harder to remove in the future.

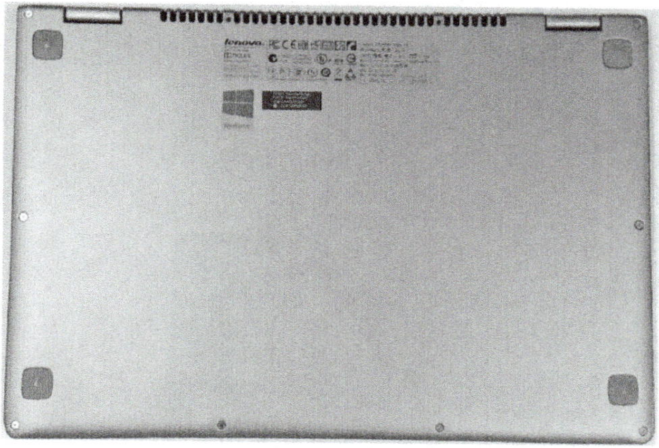

Figure 4.5 1 Piece bottom

It is common with this type of laptop that you must remove the keyboard before you can disassemble and access the RAM. So, flip the laptop over and remove the battery (if possible). Flip the laptop back over and lift the lid to reveal the screen and keyboard. With the lid open on the laptop, gently place a pry tool in between the bezel (plastic surrounding the keyboard) and the body of the laptop and slowly work your way around the keyboard with a gently lifting force to pop the keyboard up. Once the keyboard is free from the laptop, be cautious not to simply try to pull the keyboard away. There is always a connection cable of some kind that links the keyboard to the device.

Figure 4.6 Prying Keyboard Bezel

The connecting cable from the keyboard to the laptop usually come in two forms - one which requires simply pulling a blue tab on the cable to free it from its slot (never pull on the cable itself). This connection can be stressful to reconnect and may require a few attempts. However, if you take your time and be patient, it should be a breeze. The other is known as a Zero Insertion Force (ZIF) connection.

Figure 4.7 ZIF Cable

ZIF connections require you to lift a small hinged tab on the top of the connector before lifting the cable free. As the name implies, this requires very little effort to connect and disconnect. Now that the keyboard is removed, there is usually (but not always) a few screws that were previously hidden that need to be removed. As with the rest of the screws, organize and label them during removal.

Once the keyboard and hidden screws are removed, disconnect any connections you see hidden under the keyboard (certain laptops have the RAM slot right under the keyboard. If this is the case for you, simply change the chip and work backwards to rebuild the device). Now you can close the lid of the laptop and flip it over so the bottom of the device is facing upward and begin removing the remaining screws. I find it best to start from one corner and work my way around. Be sure to check under the rubber feet for hidden screws. After all the screws are removed, place a pry tool in the thin grove along the edge of the laptop and palm rest, then slowly work your way around, but do not twist the pry tool during this process as doing so will result in damage. Always be gentle and patient when using pry tools on sensitive material. You should hear a popping sound every time you release a clip: don’t worry, that is normal.

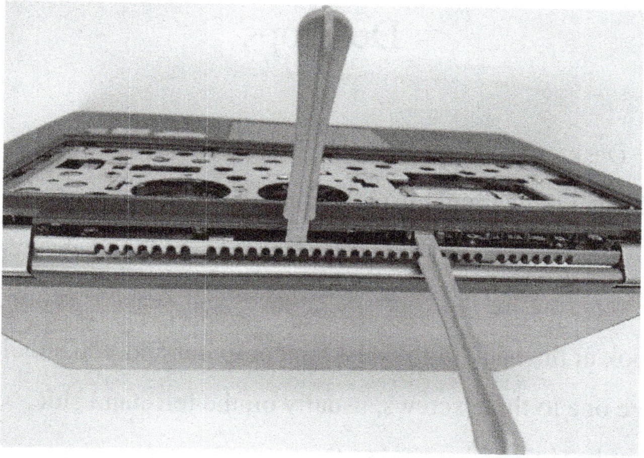

Figure 4.8 Prying Computer Apart

While prying the computer apart, be cautious of any additional connections from the motherboard to the palm rest. If any are present, gently disconnect them without forcing them from their socket. After all connections are removed, place the palm rest out of the way. Now the RAM slot should be exposed and you may proceed to add or exchange chips to achieve the amount of memory you desire. Once the chips are in place, it's best to work backwards from where you started, the last piece you removed should be the first you put back. Reassembly may take longer than disassembly.

Desktops

Desktops are typically the easiest to upgrade due to the fact they are not usually so crammed into their case. Follow the pre-upgrade instructions from above chapter "Preparing for the Upgrade". Once your space is set up, look at the back of the desktop computer and you should see one to three screws, usually on the left-hand side, that hold the side panel to the computer case.

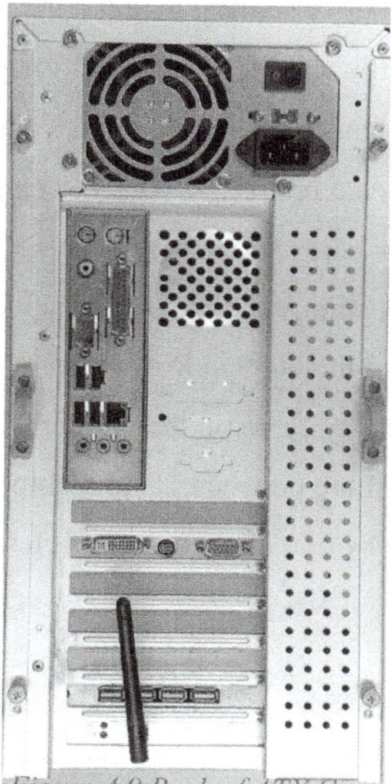

Figure 4.9 Back of ATX Case

Remove these three screws, then lay the computer onto its side and gently slide the side panel off. Set the panel out of the way, and you should now have a clear view of the inside of the computer. If you're seeing just a metal panel and a few wires then I'm afraid you've removed the wrong side; simply put the panel back on and repeat the first steps on the other side of the computer case. Locate the memory cards on the motherboard - there should be anywhere between 1 and 4 chips on the board. Each is held in by two clips, one on each side.

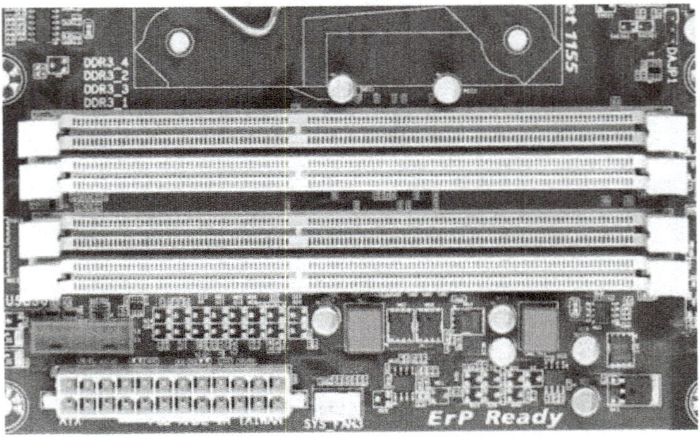

Figure 4.10 DIMM Slots

To remove the chips, place an index finger on the clips on both sides and gently push downward. There may be a clicking sound and you'll notice the chips slide up and become loose. When you grab the chips, be careful to not touch the gold contacts as you place them aside and pick up one of the new ones. Notice the notch in the gold contacts on the chip: line the notch up with the notch on the slot, then gently and evenly press the chip into the slot. The locks on both sides should move into place as the chip is pressed into the slot and repeat until all of the new chips have been added. Just remember the key word is GENTLE: trying to force chips or the locks into place will ony result in damage. Once the chips are in, you can slide the side panel back into place and secure it with the screws.

5

Learning how to care for and preserve the life of your new computer

If you have made it this far, you can make it a little further. This step may seem like the easiest but the fact is, this is the most time-consuming task of all. Not because it's difficult but because you should follow this step throughout the life of your device. Methods of care vary between different form factors and should be performed at least once a month, or even weekly to bi-weekly if the computer is in a household with smokers or pets.

Like the upgrades, we will start with the supplies needed to care for your device, then describe the process for laptops, tablets, and end with desktops.

Gathering Supplies

Before starting the cleaning process, enough work space is needed so all supplies are readily available but not in the way.

- Compressed Gas Duster: This product can be purchased from the electronics department at most stores. An air compressor regulated to 10 LBs (compressor regulators display in pounds, which is short for pounds per square inch or psi) or less will also do the trick and will not leave the chemical residue (bitterants) found in compressed gas.
- Two soft cloths: one for wet wiping, the other for dry. I prefer to use microfiber cloths because they can hold more debris then most hand cloths – however any soft cloth will do.
- Anti-static cleaner: this can also be found in the electronics department of most stores but if this is unavailable, 99% isopropyl alcohol makes a great substitute simply because it can clean most adhesives and other sticky messes, then dries within seconds. If neither are available, almost any cleaner will work if they do NOT

contain harsh solvents like ink and metal cleaners.

- Anti-static grounding bracelet: any time you're working with electronics, a grounding bracelet is a good idea. A $4 bracelet can save more money then I care to count.

Laptops

With all the supplies gathered, the first place to start is to strap on the grounding bracelet, then power down the laptop and disconnect all peripherals (keyboard, mouse, monitor, power cord, etc.). Flip the laptop over and remove the battery (if applicable). Now any bottom covers can be removed to help clear dust from the inside of the laptop. If the bottom of the laptop is one solid piece, don't worry about taking it apart.

Attach the small straw that was included with the compressed gas to the nozzle, or a fine-tipped nozzle on an air compressor. You may want to take the laptop outside to spray to prevent dust and loose debris from flying around your home. Pay close attention to vents on the case as well as the keys on the keyboard. If parts start flying off the laptop… you went too far. Spraying out the laptop shouldn't take more than a minute or two. Once done, replace any covers that were removed for cleaning but leave the battery and peripherals disconnected. Take a soft cloth and dampen it with the cleaner (remember, a little is a lot) and begin cleaning the whole laptop. I prefer to start on the lid and screen then move to the keyboard and palm rest. Do your best to get the most surface area as possible while avoiding peripheral ports (USB, display, and power ports). If you happen to get cleaner in these ports, don't panic: simply let the laptop sit unconnected for a while to let the cleaner air dry.

After each surface is wiped with the damp cloth, use the dry cloth to remove any debris remaining on the laptop. Let the laptop stand for a few minutes to air dry which will prevent any unwanted liquid damage.

Tablets / Cell Phones

Because smaller devices such as these typically cannot be disassembled, they are the easiest to clean. Begin by powering down the device and disconnecting any peripherals (USB dongles, earphones, charge cable, etc.). Use compressed gas duster or an air compressor to spray out speaker, earphone, and charge ports. Once done, dampen a soft cloth with cleaner and wipe down the device, then use a dry soft cloth to wipe away any loose debris. Let the device stand for a few minutes to allow remaining cleaner to air dry.

Desktops

Desktop computers are by far the most sensitive because the more access you have of internal components, the greater the risk of damaging those components. Before opening the case, a grounding bracelet is a must have. If you happen to shock the case itself while wearing the grounding bracelet, there is little chance of causing damage. The motherboard is separated from the actual case by brass standoff spacers. However, if you zap the motherboard there is a good chance the computer has become a very expensive knick-knack.

To begin, start by removing any disks from the disk drives, then proceed to power down the desktop. Once the device has shut down, look on the back of the case: there is usually a power switch next to the power cord. Not all desktops have this switch, but if yours does, turn the switch into the "OFF" position and disconnect the power cord. Afterwards, press the power button on the front of the computer case: this step is important because it relieves any remaining power from the system. Continue disconnecting all the peripherals (display cables, USB cables and dongles, etc.) Remove the screws on the back that secure the side panels to the body of the case on each side. Removing both sides will help blow dust and dirt out of the computer case. Using compressed gas duster, spray the whole inside of the computer case and the inner side (vents) on the side panels. Be careful of any fans inside the computer - they should be sprayed but not allowed to spin, so use something to stop free movement of fans. Whatever you use, DO NOT use a pencil or anything that contains graphite. Graphite is an electric conductor and CAN have a similar but less fun effect on a computer as a cattle prod. Tweezers or even a finger can be used to hold the fan blades in place.

Use a damp cloth to wipe the outer part of the computer case and both the front and the back of the side panels but not the inside of the case. Use a dry cloth to remove loose debris on the outside of the case (including the keyboard and monitor) and allow the computer to stand for a few minutes to air dry. Once everything has dried, reassemble the case, and reconnect all cables that were removed. Be sure to turn the power switch on the back of the computer into the "ON" position. Most IT technicians see this problem more often than severe problems. Now the computer can be powered up.

6

Figure out what to do with your old computer

In recent years, technology has made incredible advances. One of these advances is the ability to produce and market products for less, which has led to millions of computers being spread throughout the populace. With that in mind, you should realize that there may not be much return for selling your old devices, particularly if they are over three years old. Apple devices, however, retain their value longer than most other brands.

If you plan to sell your old devices, the best way to get most of its value is to sell the unit as a whole. Removing parts such as hard drives, RAM, and wireless chips have a severe impact on price and will make the device difficult to sell. Another thing to be conscious of is details. People can spot even the smallest of defects. With that in mind, I find it best to be completely honest about the item your selling and search for similar models for a fair but competitive price. Like new cars, even new devices, once used, lose a portion of their value. Try not to expect to break even on a device even if it has only been used once.

If selling the computer seems more of a hassle than it's worth or you cannot get a fair price, you can always donate old devices to charities or to someone who cannot afford a computer of their own. This is my preferred method of disposal. In my time as an IT technician, I've purchased and repaired more computers than I can keep track of. So I began finding and donating computers to younger children who need to develop computer skills and younger adults who need computers for schooling but could not afford to buy one. If there is no one you could donate old devices to, try searching the web: there are many non-profit charities that refurbish and donate computers to schools, small businesses, and kids, and some will even pay for the shipping costs. Donations can also be used for tax deductions if you obtain a receipt.

The following is a list of charities to consider:

Computers for Charities

- http://www.computersforcharities.org/

Computers with Causes

- http://www.computerswithcauses.org/

Computers4kids

- http://www.computers4kids.us/

These are just a few charities that might be interesting; if not, there are many more that might share similar goals. Another IT technician once told me he prefers to use old devices and components for target practice… and yes, shooting a computer will void RoHS compliance! *

Some of you might be worried about personal data stored on an old device, which is a reasonable concern since cybersecurity is in the highest demand. Old data does not mean you should yank out the hard drive or store the computer in the closet till "vintage" status. Removing data is relatively simple but can be time-consuming. However, even deleted data can be restored. It will help to know that most data recovery methods are VERY expensive and usually range in the thousands of dollars, so once our data are deleted, there is little chance that someone will go out of their way to recover whatever information might have been there. Data destruction, like everything else, varies greatly depending on how severely you want to keep the data out of other hands as well as which OS your system is running. I will discuss different methods of destruction in detail in the next chapter.

**Note from the Author*

RoHS compliance means a device was manufactured without the use of hazardous materials, such as lead, which is commonly used in bullets.

7

Data Destruction

I will explain varying methods by Operating System, starting with the oldest first. Additional information on removing data from different operating systems can be found online, either from YouTube or whatever search engine you prefer to use, as well as third party software that can be used to overwrite the hard drive with blank information. I will also briefly explain the difference between 32-Bit (X86) and 64-Bit (X64) operating systems, and MBR or GUID partitions.

32- VS 64-Bit

32-Bit (X86) and 64-Bit (X64) refers to the computer's CPU ability to handle information. 32-Bit can support UP TO 4GBs of RAM: therefore, you can install 32-Bit on a system with more than 4GBs RAM but it will not use any over 4GB, leaving the remainder as wasted space. If you're wondering why it's abbreviated X86, this is because ancient X86 CPUs ran 32-bit instruction sets making them compatible with 32-Bit, and the moniker just stuck. 64-Bit CPUs are beneficial due to their ability to optimize UP TO 2TB of RAM... which is an unrealistic amount of RAM for a computer, but good to know. 64-Bit OS <u>can</u> be used on systems with 2GBs or higher RAM, but still anything under 4GBs commonly uses 32-Bit.

MBR vs GUID

This references the partition of your hard drive. Master Boot Record (MBR) is the most common and is supported on hard drives of 2TBs or lower and is compatible with both legacy specs: Unified Extensible Firmware Interface (UEFI) or Basic Input/Output System BIOS (UEFI has been used in computers since 2005 and is the most common BIOS format for newer computers). Globally Unique Identifier (GUID) is used only with UEFI computer systems and is used for hard drives up to and beyond 2TBs, which is awesome for gamers who optimize RAID 5 and weirdos like me that just want to pack the living circuits out of a computer.

Windows XP

Windows XP was released in 2001, but retired in 2014. The typical lifespan of any software is three years but XP extended beyond that because it is favored by many because of its smooth operation, familiarity, and reliability. The first step before deleting any files is backing up data: one or more DVDs or a USB drive is needed to perform the backup. Backup can be initiated by clicking the Start menu, "All Programs", "Accessories", "System Tools", then "Backup". A new window will open called "Backup and Restore Wizard" click the "Next" option and from the new menu you can select the best option for your information. Once the backup is finished you can begin removing data.

The easiest method is to delete any user accounts that have sensitive information. To do this, click "Start", "Control Panel", "User Accounts", then select the account you want to delete, and click "Delete the Account", "Delete All Files", "Delete Account". If the account you're planning to delete is a system administrator, create a new account with administer privileges and delete the remaining accounts from the new blank account.

Another method is to completely wipe the drive; while this will decrease the value a LITTLE, it will retain more value than simply ripping out the hard drive. If the buyer has some knowledge of computer operating systems, they will be able to reinstall the operating system with ease if they have the software and the COA to do so. To wipe the drive, you will need an installation disc or if the computer has the feature, the recovery menu from start up. If you intend to use a disc, it does not have to be the same operating system disc that is on the computer - newer versions are typically easier to navigate. If using an XP installation disk, load the disc into the DVD drive (or USB), and restart your computer. Once the screen goes black, start pressing the key(s) to open the boot menu. Typically, it is the F8 or FN+F8 key to reach the boot menu, but this may differ depending on the brand you have (watch for the manufacturer logo on start up, there is usually a list of key start up options displayed on this menu). These may include accessing BIOS, diagnostics, and boot menu. Once the boot menu is loaded, select the platform you are attempting to reach (DVD or USB); the option you want should be labeled "Windows XP disc". Once loaded, you should see a blue screen. At this blue screen are a couple of options:

- To set up Windows XP now, press “Enter”.
- To repair Windows XP installation using Recovery Console, press “R”.
- To quit Setup without installing Windows XP, press “F3”.

From these options, press “R”. It may take a couple of minutes to load. Once loaded, you should be at a black command prompt (DOS) screen. From here, you must select which drive you want to interact with: there will be a number with a drive letter next to it (press the number to select the drive, most likely it will be number one) and press “Enter”. A command line will prompt you for the administrator account password - if you do not have one, leave it blank and press “Enter” again. Type DISKPART into the command prompt (normally this is a dangerous command to play with because it CAN be used to wipe a drive, so if that is not your intention, don’t play with it). Once in DISKPART mode, type LIST DISK, then press “Enter”. Select the disk that the operating system is held on by typing SELECT DISK (DISK NUMBER) and type CLEAN, then press “Enter”.

A new prompt should appear stating that the action has completed successfully. Type EXIT, then press “Enter” to leave DISKPART. Typing EXIT again will quit the recovery console and restart the computer. Honestly, if this is the method you're attempting, it would be just as easy and only a little more time consuming to simply install a fresh operating system over the old one. If you plan to perform this method using a newer disk, once the disk is loaded, "Shift" + F10 will open a command prompt, from there the commands are the same: DISK PART, "Enter", LIST DISK, "Enter", SELECT DISK (DISK NUMBER), "Enter", CLEAN, "Enter", EXIT, "Enter", EXIT.

Windows Vista

Vista was the successor of Windows XP but didn't fully live up to expectations. Vista was a decent OS for home use but rarely made its way into businesses due, in part, to its "pickiness" on device compatibility and key variations from XP. We all know people tend to shy away from change, and Vista sadly didn't offer enough improvements and stability for people to make that change. Its release came in 2007, six years after XP and only two years before the birth of Windows 7 in 2009.

Despite the differences in the OS itself, the process of removing user data is about the same. Start by backing up your data. To do this, place a blank USB or DVD into the computer, click the Start menu, and "Control Panel" (if you're in icon view, there will be an icon that says "System & Maintenance" and right under that, click "Back up Your Computer"). This will bring up a new window of options to choose from; select the best option for you and follow the prompts. For the target destination, where you want the data to be saved, a USB will be the fastest and safest. Once done, remove the back-up media, and continue to remove user information.

The easiest is to delete the user but if the account you want to delete is the system administrator (usually shortened to “admin”), you will need to create and use a new blank system admin account. The name of the account isn’t super important, as long as it is a system administrator. To perform actions in Vista, click “Start”, “Control Panel”, “User Accounts and Family Safety”, “User Accounts”, and “Manage Another Account”. From here you can choose to add or remove an account. If deleting the account is the goal, continue by clicking the account and click “Delete Account”, then choose to delete or keep the files. Make sure you’re on the blank system administrator before trying to delete your account. Windows will not let you delete an account that is currently logged in.

Another method is to reformat the whole drive from a boot disk. Just as with XP, you can use any installation disk or USB despite the version of OS. The process is slightly different from XP (faster and easier). Start by putting the disk or the USB into the computer, then click “Restart”. Once the computer starts up, begin pressing the boot menu key, which is usually the F8 or F12 key or a combination of FN+F8 or FN+F12. If you’re using a disk, you will come to a black screen that states “Press any key to boot CD or DVD", then do so now. You may be prompted to choose a 64-Bit (X64) or 32-Bit (X86) version of the software. If you're just going to wipe the drive, it won't matter which you choose. If you intend to re-install the software, then you should choose the version of Windows that best matches your machine. If the system has less than 4GB of RAM, 32-Bit (X86) will be the best option. Any system with 4GB RAM or higher, 64-Bit (X64) will be the best option.

Once you get to the blue "Install Now" screen, press "Shift"+F10 to open the command prompt. Type DISKPART, press "Enter", LIST DISK, "Enter". Select the disk that stores your OS by typing SELECT DISK 0, "Enter". When selecting the disk to wipe, the disk number will usually be 0 but not always: if yours is different, type that number instead of 0. You can now close the command prompt screen. If you intend to re-install the OS, simply click "Install Now" and choose "Custom Install", select a destination disk, and click "Next" to begin the install. Otherwise simply press "ESC" and the computer will restart.

If your Vista machine has a recovery partition on the hard drive, that will be an easier method than completely wiping the drive or re-installing software. To get to the recovery partition, restart the computer and select the key from the list at boot. Usually it will be F10 or F11 or a combination of FN+F10 or F11. Newer computers, however, have made F12 the recovery key. Lenovo, on the other hand, has a small button on the side near the power port or by the power button. By pressing this button, the Lenovo device will boot to a BIOS/troubleshooting menu. Once you boot to this partition, you can select to "Repair Your Computer" and from the new menu, select "Reset Your PC" and select to remove files. If you do not have the reset option, you may have to go back to the first menu and select troubleshooting or advanced options: the reset should be in one of these menus. The recovery menu typically varies in look and in options depending on the version of OS as well as manufacturer, so you may have to search awhile to find the option you want (if there is one). Because manufacturers like as many proprietary options as they can get, which makes it nearly impossible to describe every option or variables you might find from one computer to another.

Windows 7

Released in 2009, Windows 7 was, and still is, one of the most popular operating systems in both home and business applications. Ranked in the top three best operating systems for business, (XP, Linux Ubuntu, and Windows 7) it is very easy to find both brand new and older used computers running Windows 7 to this day.

Removing user data from Windows 7 is nearly identical to Windows Vista, and just like XP and Vista, start by backing up your data. Place a blank DVD or USB into the computer and click "Start", then "Control Panel" - when the window pops up, you will see an icon for "System and Security" in category view, then right under that there will be a small option that says, "Back up your computer". This will open a new page; the top half of the page will be for back up and the bottom half will be for restore. Click "Set Up Backup" and a new window will appear that says, "Select where you want to save your backup", select your backup destination and click "Next". The backup page will ask you what you want to back up and give you two options: "Let Windows choose" or "Let me choose", after which you can choose if you want to run the backup on a schedule, or uncheck the box and only run it once.

Once your data are backed up, you can begin removing them from your old computer. The simplest way is to delete your user account. Start by creating a new administrator account. To do so, click “Start”, then “Control Panel”; if you’re using category view, right under “User Accounts and Family Safety”, you will see an option for “Add or Remove User Accounts”, then click there. This will bring up a list of all the accounts on your system. Note that you cannot delete the Guest account. Click “Create a New Account”, pick a name, and select Administrator: this account will not need a password. Once the account has been set up, log onto the new administrator account, then repeat the original steps: “Start”, “Control Panel”, “User Accounts and Family Safety” (Add or remove user accounts), then click the account you want to delete. A new list of options should appear: from here you can select “Delete Account”, but you may be prompted for the account password or User Account Control (UAC: a Microsoft security feature) password for the new administrator - select to delete the account files.

Just as with the other operating systems, you can use the recovery partition on the hard drive to reset the computer to factory default (if your computer has a recovery partition, that is). To access this, restart your computer, and press the key for the recovery option at startup, which for most brands of computers is F11, though you may have to press CTRL+F11, or ALT+F10, and the computer will continue to boot to the recovery partition (these keys may take you to an Advanced Boot Options menu, from here select "Recovery"). Once here, you may have the option to reset the system right away, or you may have to select "Advanced Options", then "Reset". This recovery partition may look different depending on the brand of the computer, so you may be required to do a little searching to find what you want.

The third option is, of course, to wipe or reinstall the OS. For this you will need a Windows OS disc or USB, although it does not have to be the same version as yours unless you intend to reinstall. To begin, place the disc or USB into the computer and select "Restart". Once your computer starts to boot up, you will need to access the boot menu, typically F8, and select "Windows disk" or "USB". After a moment of loading, you will see a blue "Install Now" screen, by pressing "Shift"+F10, the command prompt will open, type DISK PART, press "Enter", LIST DISK, "Enter"; now you must select your hard drive from the list (which is typically disk 0) by typing, SELECT DISK 0, "Enter", CLEAN, "Enter", then finish by closing the command prompt window. If you are done here, press "ESC" and your computer will restart. If you intend to re-install the software, continue by clicking "Install Now", select the version of Windows to install, select the target hard drive, enter the product key, and wait for the software to finish installing.

Windows 8

This OS was developed to be part of a unified platform system, meaning the ability to be used on multiple devices (computers, tablets, phones, etc.). However, it had a very short-lived existence and was considered out of service in January, 2016 - just four years after its release date in October, 2012. Because Windows 8 computers were given a free upgrade to Windows 8.1 only one year after its release, (the upgrade remains free to Windows 8 computers to this day) and is no longer considered in service, it will not be included in this book. I personally found this OS exciting for its fresh colors and themes, however most people placed it right next to Vista as one of Microsoft's greatest flops.

Windows 8.1

Considered to be the correction of Windows 8, its release date in 2013, as mentioned above, came only one year after the release of Windows 8. While many considered it preferable to Windows 8, it was still less popular than Windows 7, with the result that most computer manufacturers offered a selecting of computers with either Windows 7 or 8.1. With its Metro Interface, Microsoft used Windows 8.1 to continue its plan of uniformity by allowing it to be installed on phones and tablets, as well as computers.

For data destruction on this OS, start with backing up your hard drive. Begin by choosing the media you want to back up your data on, which could be a USB, external hard drive, or DVDs. Place the media into the computer. With Windows 8.1, there are multiple ways of reaching the backup utility. The first method is performed by moving your cursor to the bottom right hand corner of the screen, then when the side panel opens, click "Settings", and again at the bottom right hand corner, select "Change PC Settings". After a new screen pops up, on the lower left hand side, select the option "Update and Recovery", then select "File History", and you should see an option that says, "Select a Drive". By clicking that, a new popup will open, which will allow you to select your preferred method of backup media. Once your drive is selected, turn on "File History" and select "Back Up Now". This process may take a while to complete.

Another method to reach the backup utility is to select the start menu in the bottom left hand corner of the screen, and begin typing BACKUP - you may have to click the little magnifying glass in the top right corner of the screen to begin the search. A list of options should begin to develop, at the top of which should be "File History Settings": by clicking this option, you will be taken to the same page as the first method, and must follow the same instructions to back up your drive. This method is just a little easier for those that have trouble navigating Windows 8.1. If this is the option you've chosen, don't be ashamed: many people despised the Metro-style interface, but truth be told, you can simply type in anything you're looking for at the start menu and will be given a reasonable list of options. Doing so will make this version of Windows far more pleasant for people who are not computer-oriented.

Now that the backup is complete, you can begin removing the data from the computer. The easiest method, as always, is to delete any accounts that have sensitive data. And of course, the easiest way to reach this option, is to open the start menu, and begin typing USER; at the top of the search list, you will see "Add, Delete, and Manage Other User Accounts". If the account you want to delete happens to be the one you're using now, start by clicking "Add an Account", then create the new account as a system administrator, log onto the new account, and go to the same page - from here you can select the account you wish to delete, and simply click "Delete". You may be prompted for that account's password, if there is one.

Windows 8.1 includes a very nifty feature: the ability to reset your operating system from your operating system. While that may seem too cool to be easy, it is, in fact, very simple. To begin, click the start menu, and begin typing RESET, the second from the top of the menu, will have the option to "Refresh Your PC Without Affecting Your Files" (this option is very nice if you're having trouble with your computer due to misbehaving software and various other issues) and just under that will be the option "Remove Everything and Reinstall

Windows". Despite which you select, you will be taken into the PC settings under "Upgrade and Recovery"; from here, three options will be available. Select the middle option to remove everything; depending on the UAC settings, an administrator password may be required, and Windows will display a prompt stating that "All Files and User Data will be Removed" then Windows will reinstall. While this option is easy, it will also be time consuming.

Just like the older operating systems, drive wiping and reinstalling are options - however, with the ability to reset the computer right from the Graphical User Interface (GUI), these options are made unnecessary. It is good to know that you can access the recovery partition by restarting the computer and holding F12 or ALT+F12 during boot. While unneeded for removing data, it is still useful for correcting system errors with tools such as startup repair, access to Admin command prompt, and troubleshooting. Depending on the brand of computer, the access keys may differ. If you need access to the recovery console and cannot quite find it yourself, simply search "how to access recovery console on (BRAND) computers" in your preferred search engine.

Windows 10

The newest (and some say last) operating system that Microsoft has created, Windows 10 was released in 2015. While it does seem to have the best features of both Windows 7 and 8.1, Windows 10 is unique in its own ways. On its release date, Microsoft offered Windows 10 free to both Windows 7 and 8 users for one year, which originally made people skeptical. I, of course, thought it was amazing with its sleek look, low system demands, reduction in fragmentation, and universal compatibility (ability to function on PC, tablets, smartphones, and embedded devices). Not only did Windows 10 keep the tile-styled apps from 8 but included a new personal assistant, Cortana. Cortana has the ability to set reminders, answer questions by using the Bing search engine (such as checking weather and traffic reports), and giving directions to where you want to go.

The first place to start is to create a backup: this has become very easy in Windows 10. Simply click the start menu, "Settings" (depending on your version of Windows 10, this may be a cog symbol), "Update & Security", "Backup", then insert a DVD, USB, or external hard drive into the computer and click "Add a Drive". This will bring up a list of acceptable drives for backup; simply select the desired drive and proceed to back up. If you don't want to take the long way, you can simply click "Start" and type BACKUP into the search bar.

To remove your user data, there are two methods that will be easiest: the first is to reset the OS. Click the start menu, "Settings", "Update & Security", "Recovery", and at the very top of the list will be the option to "Reset This PC". Click "Get Started" - the screen will turn gray and you will have the option to "Keep My Files" or "Remove Everything". Once you click "Remove Everything", Windows will begin the process (which does take a while) and you may be prompted that everything will be removed from the device.

Another method is to simply delete the user account. To do this, the steps are similar to resetting the PC. Click the start menu, and "Settings", but this time, click "Accounts" and notice that second to last on the list will be "Family & Other People". Once you click this, you will see a section "Other people" - from here, you can click on an account name and select "Remove". However, if the account you want to remove happens to be the account you're on, click "Add Someone Else to This PC". You will be prompted for an email or phone number, but at the bottom there is an option "I Don't Have This Person's Sign-in Information". Microsoft will try to get you to create a new Microsoft account, but at the bottom you can click "Add a User Without a Microsoft Account". Then all you will need is a user name. Make sure the account is an administrator and log into the new account, then return to the "Family & Other People" page in "Settings", then simply click the account you wish to delete and select "Remove". You may be prompted for the account's password and if you want to delete all the user's data. While this is a viable option for deleting user data, it's easier to simply reset the PC.

8

Upgrading Hard Drives

Upgrading hard drives is much like upgrading RAM, although it's not always as easy to remove and replace a hard drive as it is RAM. First, I will begin by explaining the different types of hard drives, then the components required to perform the upgrade, and finally the process of upgrading.

Note from the Author

Before any upgrade, I advise backing up data. Refer to Chapter 7 Data Destruction. Under each operating system are instructions for backing up data.

Hard Drives (HDDs)

The most common hard drives found in computers today are magnetic hard drive disks. The reason it's called a magnetic hard drive is because they contain magnetic metal platers that store information by collecting small magnetic particles discharged from the Write head. Hard drives are rated in two ways: storage capacity and speed. The higher the capacity means more surface area exists on the platers. Speed can be 5,400, 7,200, or 10,000 RPM (the RPM is how may revolutions the magnetic plater can make per minute). It makes sense that the higher RPM, the faster your Read and Write speeds will be. While it may not be a noticeable difference for a home PC, gaming PCs and servers operate better with higher RPM hard drives. A major downside to magnetic hard drives is the fragile nature of the component itself - while they have built in stabilizers, even a light tap can cause the Write head to skid across the plater causing catastrophic, and often irreparable, damage.

As well as speed and storage space, magnetic HDD these days can be found in 2 standards: Serial AT Attachment 2 (SATA2 which has a transfer speed of 3

GBs per second), and SATA3 (which transfers up to 6 GB/s). It's becoming increasingly difficult to find SATA2 hard drives, which, in fact, is in no way a bad thing.

Beyond speed and space, you will also have to consider the size. Magnetic HDD come in 3 standard sizes (though other sizes may be found for surveillance and other types of systems). The sizes are 3.5" inch HDD (commonly found in desktops and servers), 2.5" x 9MM hard drives (commonly used in laptops and gaming systems), and 2.5" x 7MM hard drives (which works the same as the 9MM hard drive, but was preferred by computer manufacturers who wanted to skim a little height off smaller devices). Even better is the fact that 7MM HDD can be placed in any 9MM slot, plus expansion adaptors can be purchased to allow a 2.5" HDD to fit snuggly into 3.5" drive bays. Be cautious, though: just because a 2.5" can be altered to fit a 3.5", the opposite is not necessarily true or false. Tech vendors have been known to make aftermarket additions to gaming systems that will allow 3.5" HDD to connect almost seamlessly into a 2.5" drive bay…almost. It's also good to know that 2.5" drives are typically a little more expensive than a 3.5", but it's ability to adapt into a larger slot will usually make it worth the price. Also note that most systems use a MBR style partition table which has a limit of 2TB HDD space: most people simply won't need or use more than 500GB-1TB of space, so there is no need to blow a full paycheck for wasted space.

Solid State Drives (SSDs)

The second most common type of hard drive found in computer systems is solid state drives. As their name implies, they have no moving parts and are composed of flash memory. While flash memory allows for faster read and write speeds and is less susceptible to physical damage, there are disadvantages: namely price. SSDs will run at about $0.24 per GB, which may not seem like much until you multiply it by 500GBs ($120 versus $50 that a 1TB magnetic HDD would typically cost). To add to the higher cost, in the event of a failure, data will be impossible to recover.

Solid state drives come in many different forms, such as USB flash drives, SD, and micro SD cards; even RAM is a form of solid state flash memory. For use as a hard drive, there are only three types you need to be aware of: 2.5", which has the same uses as 2.5" magnetic HDD (and has made a huge impact on the gaming community, in both PC and other formats);") 1.8"; and 1.2" mSATA (which are much smaller and skinnier than a 2.5" SSD, and have the same shape as mini PCIe cards, which are Wi-Fi cards found in computers). While the connectors may be identical, mSATA and mPCIe have different standards which means a mSATA will not function in a mPCIe slot, and vice versa. You're probably wondering what this type of SSD has to do with your computer. mSATA, being very small form factors, have been the latest trend in super-thin laptops and tablet computers. Like the other storage devices, mSATA is rated in SATA2 and SATA3 versions. If you intend to upgrade any version of mSATA storage, be sure to double check the systems standards to be confident it is an actual upgrade from the original.

When shopping for any type of new hard drive, be cautious of cheaper models. Western Digital is a very popular brand for magnetic HDD due to their sturdy design, high performance, and reasonable price (note that WD bases different HDD by color, some of which are not designed for Desktop/Laptop use). For SSDs, SanDisk is one of the most popular brands based on quality and price and are often sold in bundle packs at volume discounts. When it comes to computer components, price reflects quality.

Components

After you have selected and purchased the new hard drive, you will need the same tools as you had for upgrading the RAM, plus two additional items: the operating system, and a product key (the code found on a COA).

1. Grounding Bracelet (to avoid electric static discharge)
2. Mini Assorted Screwdriver Kit
3. Plastic Tweezers (metal will work if you have a grounding bracelet)
4. Compartmental Organizer (for little screws and parts)
5. Plastic Pry Tool (most people typically use an old credit card or gift card for this purpose)
6. Operating System Software (this must be the version you want; only Windows 8 can upgrade to Windows 8.1 at no additional cost)
7. Product Key (If you purchased the software from a legitimate vendor, this will be included or it can be purchased from Microsoft)

Once you have everything you need for the upgrade, set up a clean, dry workspace away from any static producing materials (such as bubble wrap and Styrofoam®); this also means do not work directly on carpet. Working in a carpeted area is fine if none of your components touch the carpet. My preferred workspace is a large desk or a six-foot foldable picnic table. Setup your supplies in a manner that makes them easily accessible but won't crowd your movement, then find a way to connect your grounding bracelet to unpainted metal, or a grounding slot on a wall outlet. The grounding slot on an electrical outlet does not have any electrical connection of its own; it is simply used to let excess current leave the circuit in a safe manner by connecting a single copper wire to a piece of unpainted metal inside the wall, so you won’t get a holy zap if you plug something into it…. if you’re using the right plug, anyway (the half oblong hole). If you manage to plug it into the wrong slot on the outlet, upgrading won’t be a concern! If you are connecting to a wall outlet, there should be no obstructions for the grounding bracelet to snag on.

Figure 8.1 Plugged Grounding Bracelet

Hard Drive Upgrade

Because of their popularity, I will first describe the process of upgrading laptops (which have two typical forms: single piece covers, and one to three piece covers), then finish by explaining desktop upgrades. Note that the process is identical to that of upgrading RAM, so upgrading both at the same time makes a lot of sense. I explained that the location for RAM is marked by a small depiction of a RAM chip; likewise, a hard drive's location is marked by a small depiction of 3 disks stacked vertically. These symbols will be very small and located on the cover that protects the component.

Always be gentle when working with expensive components: attempting to force any parts in or out of place will only result in unwanted damage.

Note from the Author

Whenever I change one of my personal hard drives, I wipe its data by booting a computer to an install disk, opening the command prompt at the "Install Now" section by clicking "Shift"+F10, typing DISKPART, press "Enter", LIST DISK, "Enter", SELECT DISK 0 (use the number of the disk you want to clean, which may be different from zero), "Enter", CLEAN, and finish by powering down the computer. This will completely wipe all data, including the operating system from the drive, making it safe to resell or reuse for other projects. This way, you won't have a useless hard drive full of personal information sitting in your junk drawer, like so many other people.

Hard Drive Upgrade
Laptops
A. Single Piece Covers

Before you begin, remove any disks from the DVD drive, then remove any peripherals (USB devices and cables), power down the device and close the lid, flip the laptop over and remove the battery. Strap on your grounding bracelet and begin removing screws then placing them in the organizer. I start in the top left cover closest to the battery; screws in this location (near the hinges) are typically longer than the other screws. If this is the case for your laptop, be sure to mark the screw's location in the organizer (hinge corners, base, DVD Drive, keyboard), as doing so will make reassembly much easier. Be sure to check under the rubber feet: there is often a screw or two hidden here, near the hinges. If you didn't find any screws but can't get the feet to re-stick, simply set them aside until later to reattach.

Once all the screws have been removed, flip the laptop back over and lift the lid. Take your pry tool and gently begin removing the keyboard, being sure to work your way around the bezel, not the individual keys. Now that the keyboard is loose, gently lift it upward to reveal the cable connections. These are usually ZIF cables, which require you to lift a little tab that holds the cable in place. There may also be connecters that require the cable to simply be pulled out or pressed in. Set the keyboard aside and notice the screws that have been revealed. Their sizes should be pressed into the metal next to them; these screws must be removed before the palm rest can be detached from the device. Be sure to carefully label these screws, as there will likely be at least two different sizes such as 2.5X3.5mm or 2X5mm.

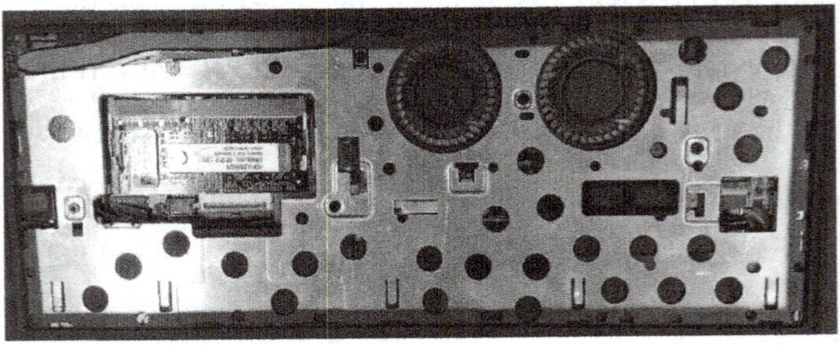

Figure 8.2 Screws Under Laptop Keyboard

Now with the lid open, start in the corner on the side opposite of the power jack and insert a pry tool in-between the palm rest and the bottom cover, then begin prying. When using pry tools, do not twist the tool: doing so will cause damage to plastic and soft metals, leaving an unsightly and permanent mark on the device. There will be a snapping sound when each clip releases.

Work around the whole of the laptop, gently lifting the palm rest away from the base, while being cautious of any cables connecting the palm rest to the motherboard.

Depending on the model of laptop, the bottom may detach from the unit rather than the palm rest. The same method is required for removal; however, the lid may need to be closed when removing the cover.

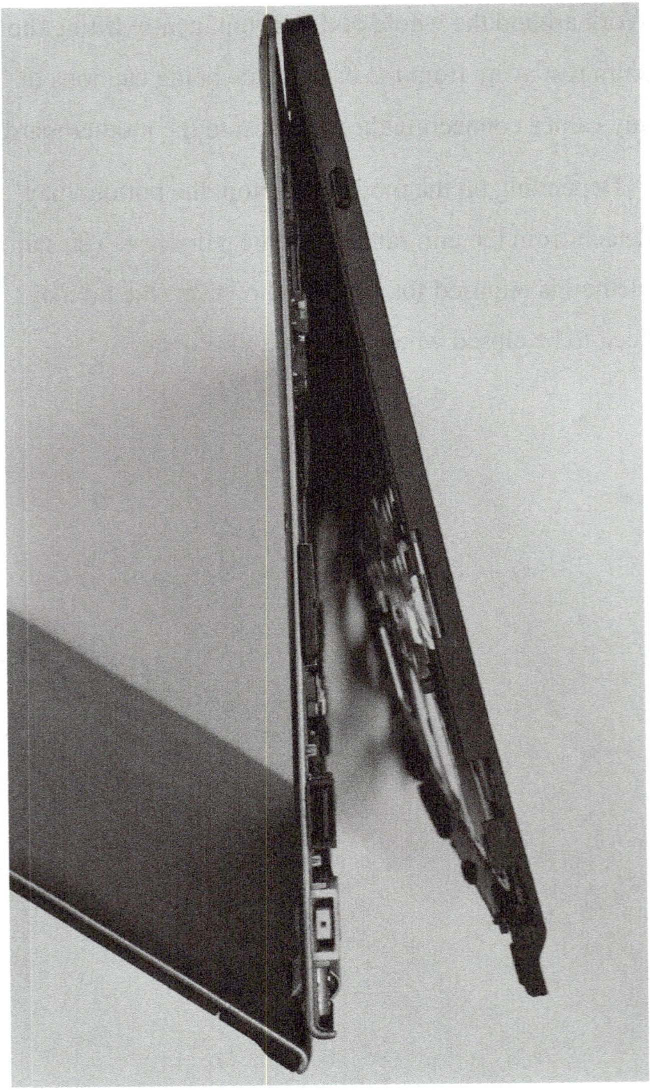

Figure 8.3 Removing Laptop Bottom

Once the cover is removed, the inner components (including the hard drive) will be exposed and held in place by a caddy. One to four screws may secure the caddy in place; begin removing the screw(s) and labeling them. Carefully slide the hard drive out of its slot, disconnect the SATA cable, make a note of the hard drive's orientation in the caddy, remove any screws that hold the caddy to the drive, then slide the drive out. With the old drive out, remove the new drive from its silver anti-static packaging and secure it into the caddy in the same orientation as the old one. Place the old drive into the silver packet that held the new one and set it out of the way. The new drive can now be connected to the SATA cable (some devices have a fixed SATA connection that simply requires the drive to slide in and out of place).

From this point, it's a simple matter of working backwards to put the system back together. There shouldn't be any extra screws once the device is reassembled. If you get frustrated or confused while reassembling, take a small break, and come back to it in a few minutes. Some people find it helpful to record the disassembly process to use for reference when reassembling. If you could not reattach the rubber feet, this can be done with double-sided tape or even a very small amount of Superglue. If the feet are Styrofoam, however, do not put them anywhere near Superglue; instead, try a small amount of epoxy because Styrofoam and Superglue are a nasty and harmful combination.

Once the device is reassembled, you will still need to install an operating system before you can use the laptop. I will explain the install process at the end of the upgrades (you can skip there now if the next sections do not pertain to your device).

Note from the Author

If you plan to upgrade RAM as well as the hard drive, read the corresponding RAM and hard drive sections and perform both upgrades at one time. Doing so will reduce risk of damaging or losing components.

B. One to Three Piece Covers

This type of laptop is becoming less popular due to trends towards slimmer, lighter computers. They are, however, easier to upgrade. Start by removing any disks from the DVD drive and remove any peripherals (USB devices and cables) then power down the device. Close the lid and flip the laptop over; on the bottom cover you will notice one to three different covers. Each cover will have small, impressed symbols that identify the components underneath: locate the cover with the symbol of three disks stacked vertically.

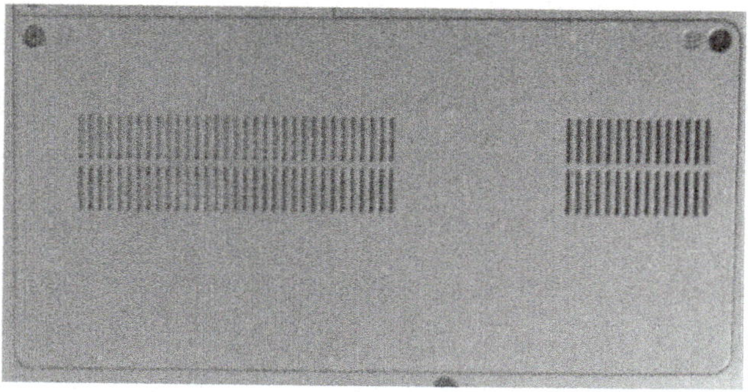

Figure 8.4 Laptop HDD Cover

Remove the screw(s) that hold this cover in place and lift to remove. There may be tabs that hold the cover in place and will require the aid of a pry tool to remove.

Once the cover has been removed, the hard drive will be revealed and secured in a caddy. Remove any screws that hold the caddy in place, lift off or slide the caddy out of its slot and disconnect the SATA cable. Some SATA connectors are fixed in place and will disconnect when the drive is slid out of place.

Before the new hard drive can go in, you must first remove the old hard drive from the caddy, which requires removing one or two screws from each side. Make a note of the drive's orientation in the caddy. Remove the new drive from its packaging and place the old drive in the silver anti-static bag from the new drive. Slide the new drive into the caddy in the same direction as the old one came out. Replace any screws that hold the drive in the caddy, connect the SATA cable or slide the drive into the SATA connector and secure the caddy in place. Re-attach the cover and lock the battery back into place. You can now flip the laptop right side up and skip to the "Installing an Operating System" section of this book if no other sections pertain to you.

Hard Drive Upgrade
Desktops

Desktop upgrades are the easiest to perform because you have a lot of space in an average ATX (full-size) case. However, smaller form factor cases such as micro ATX have been increasing in popularity because of their space saving size; micro ATX or slimline computers will be a little more time consuming to upgrade.

Regardless of size, begin by removing any disk media from DVD, CD, and floppy drives, then power down the PC. Once the system has shut down, unplug the power cable from the wall outlet, press the power button on the front of the case to relieve any power left in the system, disconnect all peripherals and power cables (monitors, mice/keyboards, USB dongles, etc.), and move the system to your working area.

ATX

On full-sized cases, remove any screws from the back of the case that secure the side panels to the chassis. With the computer standing upright, remove both side panels by applying pressure and sliding them toward the back of the case. The panels should lift off, revealing the motherboard. Before you continue, connect the grounding bracelet to an unpainted section of the case chassis - doing so will allow greater range of motion while working inside the case. Proceed by disconnecting the SATA cable from the hard drive: if the 15 pin SATA power cable is also connected to another drive, it won't hurt to disconnect both. Now simply remove two screws from each side that hold the hard drive in place and gently slide the drive out of its mount.

With the old drive out, pull the new drive out of its packaging and place the old drive into the silver anti-static packaging. When installing the new drive, be sure its orientation is correct: the logo should face upward with the SATA connectors facing the motherboard. If you're using a 2.5" drive with a 3.5" adaptor, attach the adaptor with the screws it provided, slide into position, and replace the screws that hold the drive in place. Some cases have tool-less drive bays that simply lock into place when the drive is installed. With the drive in place, simply reconnect any cables that were originally remove. There should be one 7 pin and one 15 pin SATA cable to the hard drive, plus a 7 pin and a 15 pin SATA cable or a 7 pin SATA and a 4 pin Molex to DVD and CD drives. Replace the side panels and the screws that secure the panels to the chassis. You can now reconnect all peripherals and skip to the "Installing an Operating System" section.

Figure 8.5 Inside ATX Case

Micro ATX (Slimline)

On micro ATX cases most of the process is the same as described above. Connect your grounding bracelet to an unpainted part of the case for less restrictive movement and remove the side panel on the left-hand side from the front, which may be held to the chassis by screws or clips, the bottom may come off with the side panel. Now with the motherboard exposed, you will notice immediate access to the hard drive is most likely not possible. In most small form cases, the hard drive is located under the disk drive. This procedure will require more work and closer attention on your part because different brands will have unique designs, but hopefully will have enough similarities to the process I will discuss.

Start by removing the disk drive, which often requires removing the face place to slide the drive out of the front. If your PC doesn't conceal the disk drive from the front, then the drive will slide out without removing additional panels. The front panel will simply unclip and slide off. There should be two or so exposed clips on each side of the case that need to be unlatched, then simply wiggle the cover until it can be slid off. Some models may also have a fan that must be removed before the disk drive. The fan should be held in place by one to four screws or clips. Always take a moment to inspect each component before attempting to remove any parts - getting in a hurry will only result in more work.

Once the front cover is removed, disconnect the SATA cables, pull on the tool-less clips that hold the drive in place, and slide the drive forward to the front of the case. If there are no accessible screws or clips, the drive should come out with the drive frame. With the disk drive out of the way, you will now be able to see the hard drive. For most small cases, the frame that holds the drives must also be removed. To do this, disconnect any cables from the hard drive, or if you cannot remove the cables just yet, do so after lifting the frame out of the case. Now take a moment to look around: the frame may be held in the case by a few screws, clips or just hooks that slide into place.

It may take a while but once you have the frame out, the drive can be detached by removing two screws from each side, then slide it out of the caddy - be sure to note the orientation before the drive is removed. Pull the new drive out of its packaging and place the old drive in the silver anti-static bag. Place the new drive in the caddy and secure it in place. The frame can now be placed back into the case, connect the SATA cables to the new drive. If you had to remove the disk drive, slide it back into place and reconnect its cables. Now work backwards to reassemble. The front panel should be reattached after all the drives are secured and cables connected but before the side panel. After the computer is fully assembled, you can reconnect all peripherals and continue to the “Installing an Operating System” section.

9

Installing an Operating System

This section will be useful after upgrading or replacing a hard drive, upgrading software on an old system, or if a system has problems with software and hardware compatibility.

Installing a new OS is extremely simple. For this reason, I will be explaining how to install Windows in general - different versions of OS are similar enough that the steps described will make installing other systems just as easy. If you run into trouble installing the software, YouTube can be a powerful tool. Simply search "How to install (OS name)" and there will be a list of short videos that will walk you through the process. Another useful tool on the OS media will allow you to upgrade the new software directly from the desktop of your current software. Note that this method cannot be used if you've just installed a brand new blank hard drive. I will explain the upgrading process after the process of installing new software.

Installing on a New Drive

To begin, insert the software media from a USB or DVD (If you've selected DVD, you will have to briefly power on the device to insert the disk). Power on the device and begin holding the boot menu key, which is typically F8 (but if you're not sure, there should be a list of key options at start up). Every home computer has a boot menu, so don't give up if you didn't get it on the first try.

Once you have arrived at the boot menu, a list will be presented. Select the software media to be installed, then you may be prompted by a black screen with bold white letters to "Press any key to boot from CD or DVD". After a few moments of loading, you will be presented with the "Installation" screen, which will have you select the language and keyboard layout desired. Once selected, click "Next" to reach the "Install Now" screen, click "Install". A new screen will appear with a large box in the center, the box will contain a list of available storage devices for installation (there may be only one drive available). Select the target drive to install the software on and click "Next".

Brand new hard drives may have some trouble at this point if they have not been formatted by the factory, as well as old drives that have been wiped, which can be frustrating but is easy to fix. Open the command prompt by pressing “Shift”+F10, type DISKPART, press “Enter”, LIST DISK, “Enter”, from the list select the problem drive by typing SELECT DISK 0, (the disk number may vary), “Enter”, CLEAN, and “Enter”. This process will prepare the drive for formatting. Reselect the drive by typing SELECT DRIVE 0, “Enter”, /FORMAT MBR, “Enter” - the drive will now format to a Master Boot Record partition table. The same can be done if you desire a GUID partition table by replacing MBR with GPT in the format command (note the main benefit of doing so is for hard drives larger than 2TB). You must also install the software from a UEFI drive and have a UEFI BIOS version. Attempting to install software from media or a BIOS system that does not support UEFI will typically reformat the drive to MBR automatically, thus making any space over 2TB unusable. One neat trick to use this space is to install other OS as well; Linux will have no trouble with this unused space. Just note, for a multiboot system, when installing different versions of Windows, you must install the oldest first: for instance, first Windows 7, then

Windows 8, and Windows 10. Not following the order of oldest to newest will make other versions unbootable.

If you want to install Linux alongside of Windows, you must install Windows first and Linux second (vice versa will make Linux unbootable because Windows will likely overwrite Linux's GRUB or LILO boot software). A nice workaround is to use virtual machine (VM) software such as Oracle's VirtualBox which allows you to boot other OS right from your desktop display (for more information, search "VirtualBox" in any search engine).

Once the formatting is complete, proceed to the installation process. If you plan to install other systems for a multiboot system without additional software such as Virtual Box, split the partition now by clicking "New" at the bottom of the box and enter the size, in megabytes (MB), for the new partition. Doing so now will save a headache later. Once you click "Next", the installation will begin - feel free to take a break, this process takes a while. But check in now and then: some versions will ask for the product key before the installation and some after. When entering the product key, the letters will capitalize and space automatically, so you won't have to hold shift and pound the space bar.

Before the installation process is finished, Windows will prompt a few more tasks before the software is usable, including things like picking theme colors, setting up network connections, naming the computer, and setting up Microsoft and user accounts.

Make no mistake, the entire process takes a fair amount of time and for most people, a whole lot of patience. When setting up a computer for a client, I personally like to have two full days: one for installing software and updates, and one for testing the system for any hardware defects and software bugs that may cause problems later.

Upgrading to a Newer Operating System

Upgrading is an option for those who either do not like their current software, or need newer software to meet their needs. To perform the software upgrade, you will need: software media for a newer version of Windows, a product key (which should be included with the media), and patience, for the process will take a fair amount of time. Note that not all versions are compatible for direct upgrade; Microsoft offers a free Windows Upgrade Advisor that will confirm compatibility.

To begin, start the PC and allow it to load to the Graphical User Interface (GUI). Perform a backup of the system to protect against data loss should something go wrong and then insert the install media into the computer. If Auto-Play is enabled, a dialog box will appear; select "Run setup.exe". If Auto-Play is disabled, open "File Explorer", click "This PC" and double click the DVD drive. A dialog box will appear: continue by clicking "Run setup.exe". Depending on the PC settings, the UAC may prompt for administrator action to continue. A new box will open with the option to "Install Now", there may also be an option to "Check

Compatibility Online". The startup for the installation will begin, and you may be prompted again for the option to install the most current updates now or skip them until a later time. After selecting your preference of upgrades a new box will appear with a software license agreement: feel free to read this at your leisure, then at the bottom there will be a check box to agree to the terms, which must be checked to continue.

Once again, a new box will appear with two options: "Upgrade" and "Custom". "Custom" is for a fresh install which can only be done from the boot menu, so to continue, select "Upgrade". Windows will now begin to install the new software, a process that will usually take about an hour to complete and will restart the PC a few times during the process. It may prompt for the Product Key. Once done, the PC will load to the new OS, and the installation media can be removed from the PC. The computer is now ready for use. Take a moment to review the settings as they may not have transferred from the old software. You might also find certain devices and software are not compatible with the new system but this is rarely an issue.

Updating

With the installation complete, before downloading preferred software it's best to make sure all device drivers are functioning. Device drivers are software that translate instructions from hardware to software, such as mouse clicks, prints, and all other kinds of interactions, whether seen or not.

Device Manager

There are a couple of methods for accessing the device manager. For newer systems, simply right click the start menu and select Device Manager from the list, another method is to open the RUN command by pressing the Windows key + "R" at the same time. A small box will open, type DEVMGMT.MSC in the command box and press "Enter" to launch device manager. However, the simplest method is to type DEVICE MANAGER in the search box in the start menu. Once at the device manager screen, any dysfunctional devices will be shown with a yellow exclamation point. This could mean the device does not have a compatible version of the driver for your system: by double clicking the problem device, a new window will open. Under the driver tab you will be presented with the options: “Driver Details”, “Update Driver”…, “Roll Back Driver”, “Disable”, and “Uninstall”. Typically, clicking “Update Driver…” and allowing the system to search online for the most current driver will fix the problem - however, in the few cases it does not, in any search engine, type (BRAND OF THE COMPUTER) DRIVERS, such as “HP drivers”. You will be taken to the manufacturer’s support site where you can enter information about your system (typically the model or serial number and the version of Windows being used) and the site will then produce a list of different driver versions that are used for that model of computer and the date the drivers were released (one device can have many driver revisions, so it’s best to start with the newest driver).

The process of updating drives is relatively quick, but know that when you are upgrading an older system to newer software (such as a Vista machine to Windows 10) not all components may be supported. So, despite the amount of effort, some components simply won’t work.

Another good practice is to check the driver for any devices that are malfunctioning. A driver is often easier to replace than a component, so start by uninstalling the driver from device manager. The device will disappear from the list, then click the "Action" button at the top and "Scan for Hardware Changes" - the device will reappear on the list - continue by updating the driver. The device should now function.

Faulty device drivers can also cause an error known as the Blue Screen of Death (BSOD), which sounds more horrifically terrifying than it really is. In the event of BSOD, take a picture or write down the error code displayed on the screen. Restart the PC, and during start up, access the advanced boot menu, which typically requires holding F8 and boot into safe mode. Once in safe mode, navigate to Device Manager and uninstall or rollback the driver which should have an indication of a fault. Once done, restart the PC with a normal startup boot and attempt to reinstall the driver. If a driver is not the issue, the error code can be researched in any search engine for possible solutions.

Note from the Author

In the tech world, it's a simple fact that any problems you may encounter have already happened to someone else and are described on the Internet for you to research further.

Closing

Thank you for purchasing my first book. I sincerely hope you enjoyed reading it and find it helpful as a reference for selecting, upgrading, and prolonging a computer that matches your lifestyle and budget.

-TD

Common Computer Jargon

A

Adware: Software used to display advertisements based on your search habits.

AI: Artificial Intelligence. Software designed to perform intelligent responses.

App: Application. Software used to perform particular tasks.

ATX: Advanced Technology Extended. A configuration specification used for most desktop motherboards (typical ATX motherboards are 9.5"x12").

B

Backup: A copy of documents, software, pictures, etc.; used as a failsafe against data loss.

Backwards Compatible: Compatibility with older generation systems of the same variety.

Bandwidth: A measurement of data being transferred per second; measured in MB and GB.

Biometric: Biological examination of fingerprints, retina, or facial recognition.

BIOS: Basic Input/Output System. Firmware designed to manage basic components such as time, processor and memory speeds, and boot settings.

Bit: Singular unit of information in a computer system; either a 1 or a 0.

Bluetooth: Short range communication for wireless interconnecting devices; usually ranges 10 meters (approximately 32.8 feet).

Boot: Start up process of software on a system.

BPS: Bits Per Second. Measurement of bits transferred per second.

Broadband: Internet access over a high-capacity frequency transmission network.

Byte: Equivalent of 8 bits.

C

Cache: Temporary files stored for easy retrieval later.

CMOS: Complementary Metal Oxide Semiconductor. A type of memory that retains information (BIOS and time settings) after powering down a system (requires a coin battery known as the CMOS battery).

CPU: Central Processing Unit. Also known as the processor because it processes all information across the system.

D

DDR: Double Data Rate. A fast type of RAM with four current revisions.

Desktop: A computer system designed to sit on top of a desk.

DIMM: Dual In-line Memory Module. A two-sided form of memory.

Domain: An Internet address owned by an organization or individual.

Dongle: A small device that plugs into a port on a computer.

DPI: Dots Per Inch. Measurement of quality for monitors, TVs, and dot matrix printers.

Driver: Software that translates hardware actions into software format and vice versa.

DRAM: Dynamic Random Access Memory. Faster form of RAM.

DRM: Digital Rights Management. Software designed to prevent plagiarism of data.

DVI: Digital Visual Interface. Digital video connection type (29-Pin).

E

Encryption: Coding algorithms used to protect data.

ESD: Electrostatic discharge. A sudden flow of electricity between two or more electrically-charged objects. Buildup can be caused by dragging feet on carpet, rubbing balloons together, and devices such as Van de Graaff generators.

Ethernet: Medium used to connect a computer to the Internet.

EXE: Execution; to carry out a specific command.

F

FDD: Floppy Disk Drive. A disk drive designed for floppy disks.

FAT: File Allocation Table. A file type used to store information.

Firewall: Software that blocks unwanted threats from gaining access to the system.

Flash: Reimaging of stored data.

Form factor: The physical size and shape of a piece of computer hardware.

FPS: Frames Per Second. A measurement used for graphic quality.

FTP: Files Transfer Protocol. Rules and regulations used when transferring files.

G

GB: Gigabyte. Measurement of bytes; 1 GB = 1,000 MB.

GHz: Gigahertz. Measurement of frequency in cycles per second; 1 GHz = 1,000 MHz.

GUI: Graphical User Interface. The display of software that can be interacted with by a user (often referred to as a desktop display or desktop).

GUID: Globally Unique Identifier. A 32-hexadecimal digit that acts as a unique reference number.

GPT: GUID Partition Table. A partition table that can only be used with UEFI BIOS systems and has no limitations on storage space.

H

Hard disk (drive): A magnetic disk hard drive. Physical drive.

Hardware: Physical components of a computer system.

HDMI: High Definition Multimedia Interface. Digital video interface (Transfers video and sound / 19 Pin).

HTML: Hypertext Markup Language. A system used for creating web addresses.

HTTP: Hypertext Transfer Protocol. Protocol used for accessing sites over the Internet.

HTTPS: Hypertext Transfer Protocol Security. Protocol used for accessing sites over the Internet with higher security.

I

IDE: Integrated Device Electronics. An outdated but not forgotten form of data connection; 40 pin connectors.

IP Address: Internet Protocol Address. A unique number assigned to a computer to allow Internet access.

IT: Information Technology. The technological management of information.

K

KBPS: Kilobytes Per Second. Measurement of bytes transferred per second. 1 KBPS = 1,000 Bytes Per Second.

Kilobyte: Measurement of bytes. 1 KB = 1,000 Bytes.

L

LAN: Local Area Network. Network that spans a small area such as a house or office.

M

MAC Address: Media Access Control Address. A unique identification number for a network device.

Malware: Malicious Software. General term for Spyware, Adware, etc.

MBPS: Megabytes Per Second. Measurement of bytes transferred per second. 1 MB = 1,000 Bytes.

Megabyte: Measurement of bytes. 1 MB = 1,000 Bytes.

MBR: Master Boot Record. The boot sector for a hard drive; limits storage space up to 2TB.

MHz: Megahertz. Measurement of cycles per second. 1 MHz = 1,000,000 Hz.

Megapixels: Measurement of pixels. 1 MP = 1,000,000 Pixels.

Memory: Information stored for future use. Also known as RAM or DRAM.

MicroATX: Micro Advanced Technology Extended. A smaller revision of the ATX standard.

Mobo: Motherboard. Circuit board that consists of electrical components.

N

Network: Linked computers over the same medium (modem/Internet).

NIC: Network Interface Card. Expansion card that provides network connectivity.

NTFS: New Technology File System. Proprietary file system developed by Microsoft; it provides more security than FAT.

O

OEM: Original Equipment Manufacturer. The first producer of a component.

Open Source: Software produced and distributed with little, to no, copyright restrictions (typically free).

OS: Operating System. Software that allows a user to interact with a computer (interactive general platform for software).

P

PC: Personal Computer or IBM PC. A computer designed for medium to small use duty (day to day operations, desktops or laptops); typically exclusive from Macintoshes.

PCI: Peripheral Component Interconnect. A standard for peripheral connections.

PCIe: Peripheral Component Interconnect Express A faster standard of PCI.

PDF: Portable Document Format. A compact document format that requires little drive space.

Phishing: A form of social engineering attack designed to collect information in "Confirm your details" fashion.

POP3: Post Office Protocol 3. Protocol for sending and receiving email.

POST: Power On Self-Test. A test of system components at start up and will use a beep or light code to signal test results.

R

RAID: Redundant Array of Independent Disks. The combination of hard drives to increase performance and fault protection.

RAM: Random Access Memory. Computer memory that stores information while the system has power.

S

Safe Mode: A version of the OS with the bare minimum of necessary components to function (A useful tool for troubleshooting).

SATA: Serial Advanced Technology Attachment (Serial ATA). Connection format used in computers for high speed transmission; SATA Power Cable: 15 Pin large connector; SATA Data Cable: 7 Pin Small Connector.

SIMM: Single In-line Memory Module. Outdated form of memory; replaced by DIMM.

SMTP: Simple Mail Transfer Protocol. An outdated email transfer protocol.

Spam: Unwanted solicitation in bulk.

Spyware: A form of malware that spies on the target and reports back to the attacker.

SSD: Solid State Drive. A form of storage device with no moving parts.

Start Menu: A menu of options displayed when the start (Windows button) is pressed.

T

Taskbar: The bar along the bottom of the GUI used to perform and organize tasks.

TB: Terabyte. A measurement of bytes. 1 TB = 1,000 GB.

Thumb Drive: A small thumb-sized storage device (USB drive).

Trojan Horse: A form of malware that is disguised as innocent software (often simply referred to as a trojan).

U

UEFI: Unified Extensible Firmware Interface. A newer, more advanced and interactive BIOS type (Compatible with GPT for storage space over 2TB).

Upload: to transfer data onto a network.

URL: Universal Resource Locator. An address used to locate information on the Internet.

USB: Universal Serial Bus. A connection type for high speed transmission.

V

VGA: Video Graphics Array. An older video connection standard (Analog video connection / 15 Pin).

Virus: Software designed to disrupt normal operation of a system.

Volatile Memory: Memory that is stored if power is present (erases when power is removed).

VOIP: Voice Over Internet Protocol. Standards used to make phone calls over the Internet.

W

WAN: Wide Area Network. Networks clustered together to span a large area such as a city.

Wi-Fi: Wireless Fidelity. A method of connecting devices to the Internet without physical connections.

Worm: A form of malware that spreads and reproduces without action from the user.

Z

ZIF: Zero Insertion Force. A type of IC socket or electrical connection that locks into place under a clamp tab that requires very little force for insertion.

Figure 10.1 ATX Motherboard

Table of Figures

SIMPLICITY

DISCIPLINE

VICTORY

Made in the USA
Monee, IL
04 November 2026

67375685R00085